Bangalore Blue

Bangalore Blue

Terry Kennedy

Split Shift

Other books by Terry Kennedy

- *Ludlow Fugue*
    Wampeter Press (Green Harbor, Mass.)

- *Heart, Organ, Part of the Body*
    Second Coming Press (San Francisco)

- *Durango*
    The Smith (New York)

Copyright © 2005 by Terry Kennedy
All rights reserved

Cover art by Alfredo de Batuc, "Woman with Snake," oil on paper, 1990

First Edition

A Split Shift Book

Cover design: Roger Taus

ISBN 0-9655547-3-2

Distributed by Small Press Distribution, Berkeley, California

Table of Contents

Tasting You 9
Yellow Quilt 10
My Heart Is a Sparrow 11
Suicide Night 12
Dream 13
September 14
4:40 A.M. 15
The Quilt 16
Drums 17
Boston Boxes 18
The River 22
Seizing Heaven 23
Controlling Lust 24
Tibetan Refugee Cafe 26
Our Dear Mothers' Warnings 28
For Anita and Kesher 30
Temple Meditation 32
Like Kleenex in the Pocket 33
Adjunct Faculty Meeting 34
Her Bangles 36
Soon the Torrents Will Come 37
The Village Streets 38
Divali Night 39
I Try 40
Rebirth 41
Mangoes 42
Mergence 44

Tasting You

Excessive, I leave bite marks
where soft kisses grow,
your navel becomes
my third eye.
When we make love
I hear the coconut palms
massaging the balcony,
hundreds of God's green fingers
imitating my own.
If I could,
I would simply devour you.
Instead, I taste
your name, your name, your name,
in that sudden blast
that erupts inside me
before you turn me over
and let me loose
in the Ganges
where I suck the ineffable
Kundalini straw
until I have swallowed
all of India,
Bharat of the world.

Yellow Quilt

When the first rains came
we made love on the roof
of your parents' house —

Your skin glistened
like the leaves
of the Banyan tree.

I drank new life
from your lips.
Now we have our own

secret bed
with the bright quilt,
yellow as sunflowers,

frayed with our loving.
Today when the dhobi brought it
back from the drying hut,

smelling of smoke
from the charcoal fires,
I wrapped it around myself,

flooding my heart
with joy —
And I knew

I would love you
all ways
until the very last rains.

My Heart Is a Sparrow

You are not here again —
again my bed is empty
and my heart is a sparrow
too weak to fly,
too dazed to look for food.
In the beginning of our love
you walked through storms,
your ankles sinking in mud,
you faced tigers and the cruelty
of villagers just to see my face.
After I gave you my kisses
and my body, white as plumeria,
you said you would never leave me —
"How can I go away for 30 days,"
you once joked, "I can't be parted
for 30 hours."
Now you are far away from my arms
and my tears cannot sway you,
for you are no longer here to dry them.
I want to die,
but my heart is a sparrow
too paralyzed to move.

Suicide Night

Dear Heart,
The moon is too full. The crickets are too happy —
Everything is screaming your name.
I am mad with grief.
I cannot eat. I cannot sleep.
I have touched each small space
where you have stood, sat, lain —
But I cannot make you appear in my arms.
I want to die.
I want to die.
I must die.
In four nights my life will be over —
a bad dream
that ends when you put the tali
around her black neck.
God, forgive my fury —
But since I cannot let you go
entirely into her heart,
I will kill myself
and take your heart with me
while it still belongs to me only.
I know I promised to live,
to meet you on the 4th,
but, like you,
I am breaking my promise.
I will be in Yama's arms
watching you in hers.

Dream

Last night I dreamed
you were with her.
You kissed her lips,
parted her legs,
entered her body . . .
I was in a hotel
calling my mother,
begging her to help me.
She admitted she didn't know how to
cut off my love for you . . .
"Run away," she said —
and I hung up the phone
then rushed to the door
trying to make it open,
but I was too scared to make it work.
I woke up screaming, your name
caught in my throat —
the way I used to shudder
and moan
when you loved only me —
my hand on the door
could not decide
which way to go.

September

Grief you cannot imagine —
If you were feeling it
you would rise from the dead
and return to me.

Outside, the merciless rain
slips down the leaves
of the coconut trees.
Monsoon lust washes
the garden
and the Christmas pine.
The Shiva Lingam glistens
as if licked by 1,000 tongues.
O, God, how can I suffer
this separation?

Yesterday we made love
as if the world depended
on our joy.
Today the house screams
for your smile.

I hate everyone
and everything that ever held your attention,
stealing our last breaths,
nights, days. O, God,
these mornings!

4:40 A.M.

Monsoon rains pour down
swallowing me up into the belly
of despair.
Your hands, thousands of miles away,
move around my waist,
your lips sprinkle out-of-control lust
throughout my body.
What can I do but wail
and cry out
your name to the gods
of thunder, of lightning?
All alone on the yellow quilt
that was our nest
for years
I touch myself to see if I am still alive.

The Quilt

The quilt cried out in ecstasy
when we lay on her yellow fluff.
She purred like a huge cat
under our naked bodies —
How many weeks has she waited
on the bedroom shelf,
patient as a nun?
But today she was an entire planet
softening the blows
of life — and snuggled together
on her warm skin,
we, too, were Satchitananda . . .
Ah, Love,
today the yellow quilt
was satisfied.

Drums

What is the difference
between the marriage drums
and the burial drums?
This morning, without you
in our bed,
the sound was the same.

Boston Boxes

1.

Boston boxes full. 40 years of unpublished writing arriving like coffins by courier service. Beach-rose memories scent the Indian desert. I am only one of the ghosts.

I could have been receiving white lilacs from Philip — he sent them in long slim boxes whenever I ran away and he found out where I was. Did I leave clues? Wide-open red tulips exposing black centers? Jacaranda blossoms pointing north?

Once after a poetry-workshop class (that's what they were called) at the Radcliffe Center for Women's Studies in Cambridge (O! how we tried!) Margery Cavanaugh said white lilacs symbolized death to the Persians. But I liked the whites more than the purples. Another clue?

For a long time Philip's flowers were my favorites. Maybe it coincided with the height of my east-coast poetry life — or the suppression of it. This happens when you fall deeply in love. It happened with me and with Philip.

But for awhile — maybe two whole years (lifetimes), I couldn't get enough of white lilacs arriving in long, slim boxes — like Boston arriving yesterday at my front door.

2.

Funny how I can draw whole love stories of my life around flowers. Actually, when I think about it, I was probably more deeply connected to the flowers — their resilience, their infinity, their bloom-rest-bloom cycles than to the men.

First flowers — first love — for a female — May flowers for Mary, the Mother of Jesus. I understand her more than her son who, according to the elementary school nuns, preached peace and compassion but didn't do anything resembling "man's work." I saw him more as a woman and a victim of men — the picture above our kitchen table showing the long hair and so much blood.

Why did we have to crouch and eat under that horror? Mary, in the month of May, never answered. She was too pure — like the May flowers I picked for her. Jesus, I knew, could not save me from the rapes. But if I could have given him flowers then — which I could not bring myself to do, I would have given him lilies of the valley — they look like white bells — elfin and safe, hidden under the taller plants. (If he was God, why didn't he just save himself?)

3.

First husband — cherry blossoms. We planted two trees in our Duxbury garden then divorced before we saw the pink petals shower onto the O! so perfect lawn. Maybe the children picked the cherries. Could this explain their distaste for me?

Second husband — bearer of lilacs — never died as he so often swore would happen if I went permanently away. He just went out like a candle. Is this a clue?

Third husband, he brought me one bouquet of mixed wilds on our first date. He was practical. Later I called it cheap.

Then I discovered the fragrance of plumeria, as exotic as the grace of God. I fell into it — again — put down far-reaching roots. For seven steady years plumeria blossoms fell from my trees like twirling stars onto the holy ground where I walked to test my new feet — determined, actually, not to run, but to dance! This is a clue. (At the time I did not know his wife's favorite flower was jasmine.)

Imagine the dream within the dream showing me the hands of angels unwrapping the clear cellophane from my feet, new feet! And everywhere the aroma of marigolds. After the cellophane dropped away, I wanted to test my new feet.

The scene shifted as scenes within dreams within dreams can do. Two men in love with me. Me between them at a bar. (Who was paying for the drinks?) Me about to tell both of them, 'Listen up, Jerks, I don't love either of you. I love me!'

4.

And inside of my corporeality (I was very real even in this dream) this great determination — I'm different on my two, healed feet. I can stand on my own at last — the Boston Boxes proof — at least to me — that the dead are never that — and for the first time I have flowered — become the flower — Queen of the Night — that narcotic botanical wonder I first smelled on my way home from the temple one Puttaparthi midnight — that ineffable fragrance I never could quite describe or find out more about living in this village, so far away from libraries, horticulturalists, people who care about such night-blooming beauty, the civilized world ... but flowering, nevertheless, flower ... flow ...

Boston boxes. 40 years of unpublished writing arriving like coffins by courier service — Beach-rose memories scent the Indian desert. I am only one of the ghosts.

The River

After the snows melt
not even the Gods try to control
the wild river
as it sweeps through
crowded villages
and the banks of the hermit's cave.
When the waters are low
and small children can cross
the once-deepest parts,
collecting stones as pink as roses,
the Gods still refuse to tamper
with the flow.
So, who am I
trying to control this little creek
that is my life?

Seizing Heaven

When will buffalos roam
past my door again
in this India
of my heart's fulfilled desire?

When will coconut-tree branches sweep
like giant fish
across my verandah
and the terrace again?

Let me seize this heaven
by the divine testicles,
let me make love
to the very stars.

It is enough,
dear God;
it is enough.

Controlling Lust

Amen. Amen. Amen.

Last night I sat with three male pilgrims
in the holy mountains of North India
where God breathes clouds of white smoke
and eagles dart in and out of his nostrils.

The pilgrims talked of subduing lust,
conquering it with the power of prayer,
the might of will, the passion for liberation . . .
Everything female awake in me,

I listened with the ears of Mary Magdalene.
Meantime, my mind took me walking
around the lake, there I could find him
brown and stunning, his eyes

Like blades slicing my skin.
On his bed I would open
without hesitation, quick and moist,
the summer's first peony.

This morning, I saw him,
my body a dry sponge
longing for its sea.
Tonight I will lie to the pilgrims

and say I have conquered my lust
because this is what they want
me to tell them.

Meanwhile, I will spin my prayer beads
between my fingers
with the vigor of a thousand nuns.
But I will be pleading with God to appear

in the form of a Rock and Roll lover,
dancing like Shiva
on the Himalayan slopes
of my sacred body.

Ah, men. Ah, men. Ah, men.

Tibetan Refugee Cafe

I drink tea in the Tibetan refugee cafe,
smoking Indian cigarettes,
thinking about my youngest son
born this month three decades ago.

A picture of the Dalai Lama
is nailed above the cash counter.
Flies roam around the rim
of my table — they too search
for the nectar of life.

I am a sort of refugee also,
having trekked the thousands of miles
between my last life
and this one.

I would like to tell my son
of the dangers, this path
away from him leading me back
always to the dream time
of our first home.

Golden-haired and fragile,
he was never afraid
of the dark or the deepest waters,
never afraid of the ski jumps
champions would not tackle.

In two months he will marry
the girl with the coffee-colored hair,
eyes like the eyes of crows —
Like me, he will succumb to that
greater love, to that
greater marriage;
for like fire, the Truth ignites
his veins.

Yes, one day he will flee
and take refuge
under the wings of his God.
And surely, here in these Himalayan mists,
he too will find flies
longing, like monks, for liberation.

Our Dear Mothers' Warnings

We are growing,
not old,
but immortal
in the artificial light
of the Gateway Hotel —
Bangalore's home place
for the lost.

We remember other Saturdays —
football fields
and majorettes leading
the high school band
toward a different kind
of victory.

Now the lounge
echoes with memories
of our dear mothers' warnings.

The beer is good
as are the words
we speak, the news
of God walking the earth
excites us.

Outside the dusty windows
trees shake off dead leaves.
Invisible winds
lift the yellow plastic bag
caught on the matrimony vine,
and for an instant we are deluded.

Nothing stays
as it first appears —
We are the very strangers
our dear mothers' warnings
set us against.

For Anita and Kesher

"A 16-year-old girl from Aurangabad was stabbed by her father after she refused to leave her boyfriend, Kesher, who she had secretly married. Her condition is critical and the young man has fled . . ."
Times of India

. . . into the heart of terror.
Oh, sweet lovers,
what can I do but pray
God will reunite you?

What can I do but beg
for speedy remedies?
Your pain has become my own.
I long for your success —

Oh, sweet Indian Romeo and Juliet,
God cares not that you are Hindu, Anita,
or that you, Kesher, call him Allah.
We are all One
in this kingdom come.

So, Anita, tell the doctors to save you,
plead with God to carry your lover on jet legs
to your hospital bed.

Let Kesher disguise himself
as a nun,
a pujari in saffron dress,
and when he comes
let your lips touch
and explode the myths
that keep us untrue
to ourselves.

Oh, sweet forever souls,
I am praying intensely,
so hold to your dream!
Don't let go!
Know that True Love, yes
True Love,
outlives us all.

Temple Meditation

Three monkeys playing
on the temple gate,

one priest offering
fire to 335 million stars,

lonely bells piercing
my iron heart,

your patchouli skin
on the wind.

Like Kleenex in the Pocket

We always carry the dead
whether in dreams
or at the movies.

Like Kleenex in the pocket,
I.D. cards in the wallet,
they are closer to us than breathing.

Sometimes we ride on trains
across from pregnant women,
aware of the freight,

the inevitable cargo —
It is the dead,
really the dead

who possess us.

Adjunct Faculty Meeting
Rancho Santiago College, Santa Ana, California

We worked hard
every summer,
went to the top,
got good grades
under the stare
of plastic-covered fluorescents,
the sun
warming the walls
around our concrete yards.

You could see
we were poor, almost 99.9% pure
white. Grey hair flying out
at the temples. Shoes scuffed,
heels worn down
on pumps, on boots,
still shuffling,
smiling like whores,
at the adjunct faculty meeting,
filling out the soulsell forms.
No IRA, no benefits —
just chocolate chips
from the Culinary Arts Department
cookies. Eyes straining
from behind bargain-special glasses,
we sign away our hearts.

Low in the sky
a yellow ghost moon floats
above the Administration Building
as we wait —
like inmates —
for our fall assignments.

Her Bangles

Her bangles make music as she glides past me
over noon's hottest road.
Is her teenage body aware of the rain clouds
taking shape east of the mountains?

I stand in the shade
of the banana tree's umbrella
remembering the rustling silks,
remembering how my feet once raced

through the gushing torrents
flooding the streets
on the way to Your door —
my wrists as bare then as now.

Soon the Torrents Will Come

The night sky turns to purple satin
as I make my way to the Ganesha statue.
There I will ask that my own wisdom
remove every obstacle that keeps me from You.

Coconut juice trickles down the pathway
and I want to touch Your hair.
On the way past the mandir
the fragrance of jasmine stops me.

When will You acknowledge this yearning?
Monsoon winds lift up the feathers of doves
and grains of sand bite my ankles
as I hurry deeper into the darkening shadows.

How many years has it been?
Where do You keep my letters?
Soon the torrents will come
but the flame of this Jyothi will grow

even brighter.

The Village Streets

She walks through the village streets
dressed in the orange robes of the renunciate.
To those who ask, she says she is God.
For those who don't, she creates on-the-spot curses,
hurling them like hand grenades
into their purses.
On inquiry, I found out she came from Australia,
a country I have never regarded as strange.
Maybe she really is God,
as she says,
or God does not exist,
and we are all deranged.

Divali Night

On Divali night
you don't see me
inhabiting your garden
where you set out the festival lamps,
placing them all around the entrance door,
protecting your home and family
from whatever is evil.
Your wife is walking so close to you
I can feel her breath
on my neck.
On the exact spot
where you ran your tongue
only days before
you gave me up
like a bad habit.
Maybe God accepts your good-husband act,
I do not —
Meantime, I am wearing black
merging with the dark,
and I pray — as intensely as I love —
so surely my words, like fireworks,
will explode this void.

I Try

I try to meditate.
I try to repeat the name of Ram.
I try to control my senses.
But all I can do is stretch out
on the operating table
of my floor mat
counting the withering petals
of the plumeria you gave me.
Your letters,
under my pillow,
used to be a kind of sedative —
Now, the more I read them,
the more restless I become.
Beneath me the floor is cool and smooth
like your skin against mine.
Outside, the same crescent moon
that slices into me like a scalpel
shines above your door harmlessly.
I try to meditate.
I try to repeat the name of Ram.
I try to control my senses.
But all I can do is feel you
inside me.

Rebirth

I gather up all the volumes
from the past
and crush them into a small paper ball
that I roll, like a ladoo,
off the edge of the world.

This tabula rasa,
unscented, untouched,
is Yours to script
as You wish —
Whoever I was has disappeared.

In my mirror
I line Your eyes with khol,
in my bath
I anoint Your body with oil,
the nipples new

as lotus buds.

Mangoes
A ghost haunts the hills
surrounding the ashram
where we have come to be with Sai Baba.
But the Chitravathi breezes distract us,
ruffling our sarees,
hung like walls around us.
So we suck on mangoes
talking of men,
muffling our laughter.

Then, suddenly, Judy grows too serious,
whispering the name of her lover,
telling me how in Bangalore
he covered their bed with the petals of roses,
pink as virgin blood,
on their last morning together.

She looks at me
with eyes like keys,
but I keep you safe,
locked in my heart,
while I suck my mango purposefully,
letting the juice run down my chin.

Next day,
on the way to the temple,
we cross your path.
"Who is that man?"
Judy wants to know.
What man? I say,
pretending not to see you,
my tongue still tasting the mangoes.

"The one who takes your breath away
everytime he walks by;
the one you never mention
when we talk of love,
the one inside your mangoes. . . ."

Now it is nearly 3 a.m.
and Judy has not come home
from another trip to Bangalore.
I lie awake thinking of you
sleeping beside your wife —
Meanwhile, the fragrance of mangoes
is flooding the tent,
but I am swallowing thorns.

Mergence

After three years of yearning,
see-sawing between hell's deepest pits
and heaven's highest heights,
I'm resting in that in-between place
where the butterfly of love flutters
and the spot light never goes out.

Meanwhile, magnet men ignore me;
but Sai Baba attracts me,
reeling me toward Him,
capturing me like a fish
lured by its own destiny.
The Scriptures of every religion say I am a river

who has lost its way to the ocean,
that tomorrow I will be the sea itself.
But I tell you,
I am only ether,
the very breath of the Beloved.
This much I know

from my own experience,
this much is undeniable.
Bodied, disembodied,
the longing is the mergence.